Relax, God is in Charge

humor and wisdom for living and loving life

⬛ HAZELDEN®
Keep Coming Back

Created by Meiji Stewart

Illu  dell

Relax, God is in Charge
© 1997 by Meiji Stewart

ISBN# 1-56838-377-0

Hazelden
P.O. Box 176
15251 Pleasant Valley Road
Center City, MN 55012-0176
1-800-328-9000
www.hazelden.org

Illustration: David Blaisdell, Tucson, Arizona
Cover design: Kahn Design, Encinitas, California

Dedicated to my family, who mean the world to me:
My beautiful wife, Claudia. My daughter, Malia and step-son
Tommy. My mother, Nannette, and father, Richard, my
grandmother Mary, my sister, Leslie, my brothers, Ray and
Scott, my nephews and nieces Sebastien, Emilie, Skye, Luke,
Jake, Jessie Nannette, Cairo and Kamana, and to Fumi,
Jocelyne, Richard, Julie, Tom and Stephen.

Thanks to:
David for the wonderful illustrations. I am truly blessed to be
able to work with him. Thanks also to Roger and Darryl for
putting it all together, almost always under deadline (usually
yesterday). Thanks to Jeff for the delightful book covers, and,
even more, for his and Pete's friendship. Thanks to Zane,
Regina, Jan, Gay, Jane, and Neill for all you do and for being so
loving and caring. And a very special thanks to my mom and
dad for encouraging me to believe in and pursue my dreams.

God loves you... God loves you...
God loves you...

4

God's grace is so bright. I have to wear shades.

God shall be my hope, my stay,
my guide and lantern to my feet.

William Shakespeare

When I asked for all things, so that
I might enjoy life. . . I was given
life, so that I might enjoy all things.

The will of God will never take you to
where the grace of God will not protect you.

With all the infinite possibilities
of spiritual life before you, do not
settle down on a little patch of
dusty ground at the mountain's
foot in restful content. Be not
content until you reach the
mountain's summit.

J. R. Miller

No trial would trouble you if you
knew God's purpose in sending it.

The task ahead of us is never as great as the power behind us. *Ralph Waldo Emerson*

Every happening, great and small,
is a parable whereby God speaks to us,
and the art of life is to get the message.

Malcolm Muggeridge

God hath not promised Skies always blue, Flower-strewn
pathways all our lives through; God hath not promised
Sun without rain, joy without sorrow, peace without
pain. But God hath promised strength for the day, rest
for the labor, light for the way, grace for the trials, help
from above, unfailing sympathy, undying love.

Annie Johnson Flint

Call on God, but row away from the rocks.

Indian proverb

You who have received so much love
share it with others. Love others the way
that God has loved you, with tenderness.

Mother Teresa

People, places, and things were never
meant to give us life. God alone is the
author of a fulfilling life.

Gary Smalley and John Trent

12

God and I are enough.

Each one of us is God's special work of art.
Through us, he teaches and inspires,
delights and encourages, informs and
uplifts all those who view our lives.

Joni Eareckson Tada

The purpose of play is to go out and be happy...
to lay down cares and have fun for a while.

William Dorn

God loves me when I work and when I play.

Our weakness becomes strength when we
depend upon God to carry the heavy end.

Joe R. Barnett

When you come to the edge of all the light
you know, and are about to step off into
the darkness of the unknown, faith is
knowing one of two things will happen:
There will be something solid to stand on
or you will be taught how to fly.

Barbara J. Winter

It was meant to be.
God is redirecting you.
Something good will come of this.

Rose Siegel

We turn to God for help when
our foundations are shaking,
only to learn that it is God
who is shaking them.

Charles C. West

God has put into each of our lives a void
that cannot be filled by the world. We
may leave God or put him on hold, but
he is always there, patiently waiting for
us. . . to turn back to him.

Emilie Barnes

When we are away from God,
he misses us far more than we miss him.

Ruth Bell Graham

If you feel far away from God, guess who moved?

God loves you as you are,
but too much to leave you as you are.

God says no a lot but all he
is really saying is wait—
there is something better for you
down the road.

God never closes a door without opening another.

Each one of us is encircled by the presence of Almighty God.

Charles Stanley

Trust in God.
Believe in yourself.
Dare to dream.

Robert Schuller

I know not what the future holds,
but I know who holds the future.

How wonderful it is that nobody
need wait a single moment before
starting to improve the world.

Anne Frank

Hide not your talents, they for use were made.
What's a sundial in the shade?

Benjamin Franklin

What we are is God's gift to us.
What we become is our gift to God.

Walk with God
and you'll always reach
your destination.

If you knew Who walks beside you,
fear would be impossible.

A Course in Miracles

Whoever you are, whatever you do,
wherever you go, remember, God loves you.

For it is in giving that
we receive.

Saint Francis of Assisi

We cannot hold a torch
to light another's path
without brightening
our own.

Ben Sweetland

28

A candle loses nothing of its light by lighting others.

There are four things in which every man
must interest himself. Who am I? Wherefore
have I come from? Whither am I going?
How long shall I be here? All spiritual
inquiry begins with these questions
and attempts to find out the answers.

Diana Baskin

To understand everything is
to forgive everything.

Guatama Buddha

A life is not important except in
the impact it has on other lives.

Jackie Robinson

We realize that what we are
accomplishing is a drop in the ocean.
But if this drop were not in the ocean,
it would be missed.

Mother Teresa

You pray in your distress and in your need;
would that you might pray also
in the fullness of your joy and
in your days of abundance.

Kahlil Gibran

When I have a problem I pray about it, and
what comes to mind and stays there I assume
to be my answer. And this has been right so
often that I know it is God's answer.

J. L. Kraft

Let prayer be the key of the
morning and the bolt at night.

Philip Henry

Life is a flame that is always
burning itself out, but it catches fire
again every time a child is born.

George Bernard Shaw

The most important thing in the world is that
you make yourself the greatest, grandest, most
wonderful loving person in the world because
this is what you are going to be giving to your
children—to all those you meet.

Leo Buscaglia

Every child is God's own unique creation,
created for a special purpose.

My life is my message.

Mahatma Gandhi

Wake up with a smile
and go after life.
Live it, enjoy it, taste it,
smell it, feel it.

Joe Knapp

36

God gives us faces; we create our own expressions.

Each one of us is God's special work of art.
A painting like no other in all of time.

Joni Eareckson Tada

The truth about you is so lofty that
nothing unworthy of God is worthy of you.

A Course in Miracles

I am a masterpiece created by God.

I do not ask to walk smooth paths nor bear an easy load. I pray for strength and fortitude to climb the rock-strewn road. Give me such courage and I can scale the hardest peaks alone, and transform every stumbling block into a stepping stone.

Gail Brook Burket

God gives us always strength enough, and sense enough, for every thing he wants us to do.

John Ruskin

I know God will not give me anything that I can't handle.I just wish He didn't trust me so much.

Mother Teresa

Dare To...

Ask For What You Want

Believe In Yourself

Change Your Mind

Do What You Love

Enjoy Each And Every Day

Follow Your Heart's Desire

Give More Than You Receive

Have A Sense Of Humor

Insist On Being Yourself

Join In More

Kiss And Make Up

Love And Be Loved

Make New Friends

Nurture Your Spirit

Overcome Adversity

Play More

Question Conformity

Reach For The Stars

Speak Your Truth

Take Personal Responsibility

Understand More, Judge Less

Volunteer Your Time

Walk Through Fear

Xperience The Moment

Yearn For Grace

be **Z**any

Dare to follow to your heart's desire.

May God steal from you—
all that steals you from Him.

Rabi'a Al-Adawiyya

Love all God's creation, the whole and
every grain of sand in it. Love every leaf,
every ray of God's light. Love the animals,
love the plants, love everything.
If you love everything, you will
perceive the divine mystery in things.

Fyodor Dostoyevsky

There is no higher religion than service.
To work for the common good
is the greatest creed.

Albert Schweitzer

When your life is filled with the desire to see
the holiness in everyday life, something
magical happens: ordinary life becomes
extraordinary, and the very process of life
begins to nourish your soul!

Rabbi Harold Kushner

Something wonderful, something hidden.
A gift unique to you. Find it.

Ralph Waldo Emerson

Joy comes from knowing God loves
me and knows who I am and where
I'm going. . . and that my future is
secure as I rest in him.

Dr. James Dobson

God loves me <u>exactly</u> the way I am.

Hold your head high, stick your chest out.
You can make it. It gets dark sometimes
but morning comes....Keep hope alive.

Jesse Jackson

The world is round and the place
which may seem like the end
may also be only the beginning.

Ivy Baker Priest

48

No matter what is happening in your life,
know that God is waiting for you with open arms.

God made you as you are
in order to use you as He planned.

S. C. McAuley

We have been in God's thought from
all eternity, and in His creative love,
His attention never leaves us.

Michael Quoist

We are all God's children.

Miracles happen to those
who believe
in them.

Bernard Berenson

Beware what you set your heart upon.
For it surely shall be yours.

Ralph Waldo Emerson

God has a purpose and plan for my
life that no one else can fulfill.

Prayer is not an old woman's idle amusement.
Properly understood and applied,
it is the most potent instrument of action.

Mahatma Gandhi

Oh, what a cause of thankfulness it is that
we have a gracious God to go to on all
occasions! Use and enjoy this privilege
and you can never be miserable.
Oh, what an unspeakable privilege is prayer!

Lady Maxwell

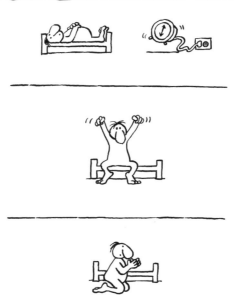

Every morning I spend fifteen minutes filling my mind full of God; and so there's no room left for worry thoughts.

Howard Chandler Christy

Somewhere on the great world the
sun is always shining, and just as
sure as you live, it will sometime
shine on you. The dear God made it
so. There is so much sunshine we
must all have our share.

Myrtle Reed

The world is charged with
the grandeur of God.

Gerard Manley Hopkins

An optimist goes to the window every morning and says, "Good morning, God." The pessimist goes to the window and says, "Good God, morning!"

Silence is not a thing we make; it is something into which we enter. It is always there. We talk about keeping silence. We keep only that which is precious. Silence is precious, for it is of God. In silence all God's acts are done; in silence alone can his voice be heard and his word spoken.

Mother Maribel

There is but one thing in the world really worth pursuing — the knowledge of God.

R. H. Benson

God is the friend of silence.
Trees, flowers, grass grow in silence.
See the stars, moon, and sun,
how they move in silence.

Mother Teresa

It is such comfort to drop the
tangles of life into God's hands
and leave them there.

Keep your faith in all beautiful things;
in the sun when it is hidden,
in the Spring when it is gone.

Roy R. Gilson

All I have seen teaches me
to trust the Creator for all I
have not seen.

Ralph Waldo Emerson

Remember, God loves you.

God bless all those that I love;
God bless all those that love me;
God bless all those that love those that I love
and all those that love those that love me.

In the name of God,
stop a moment, cease your work,
look around you. . . .

Leo Tolstoy

When you see God in everything,
God will look back at you through everything.
Ernest Holmes

On a garden wall in Peking, China, was a brass plate about two feet long with these words: Enjoy yourself. It is later than you think! Well, maybe it is later than you think; why don't you do something about it?

Charles W. Miller

What I admire in Columbus is not his having discovered a world, but having gone to search for it on the faith of an opinion.

Anne-Robert-Jacques Turgot

God promises a safe landing but not a calm passage.
Bulgarian Proverb

Our job is not to straighten each other out,
but to help each other up.

Neva Coyle

Let God love you through others
and let God love others through you.

D. M. Street

Inside every human being is a God in embryo.
It has only one desire — it wants to be born.
Kahlil Gibran

How we live, how we feel, what we think and what we become all depend on personal decisions. You are the master of your life. You can choose to celebrate life, live fully and live healthfully. Health is a choice! Happiness is a choice! Peace is a choice! And enthusiasm is the elixir that generates change, nourishes the body and feeds the soul.

Susan Smith Jones

Reach up as far as you can,
and God will reach down all the way.

John H. Vincent

Sometimes when God says 'No', it is because
God has something better in store for you.

Loving Families...

Accentuate the positive

Balance work, rest and play

Communicate with mutual respect

Don't sweat the small stuff

Encourage healthy habits

Find ways to say "I love you"

Grow self-esteem and self-acceptance

Help each other do for themselves

Inspire individuality and interdependence

Juggle schedules to "be there"

Know there are no "perfect" families

Look for the best in each other

Make the world a better place

Nurture abilities and talents

Openly talk about whatever's up

Provide safety and security

Quickly mend fences and move on

Remind each other of their greatness

Savor memories and traditions

Take time to really listen and care

Understand how precious family time is

Value presence more than presents

Work things out compassionately

Xperience life's ups and downs together

Yearn to bequeath a spirit of reverence

Zest to create a happy home

© Meiji Stewart

70

God threw a party the day you were born.

We must lay before him what is in us,
not what ought to be in us.

C. S. Lewis

Learn to get in touch with silence within
yourself and know that everything in
this life has a purpose. There are no
mistakes, no coincidences, all events are
blessings given to us to learn from.

Elizabeth Kubler-Ross

72

W. C. Fields, a lifetime agnostic,
was discovered reading a Bible on
his deathbed. "I'm looking for a
loophole," he explained.

One of the most wonderful things about
knowing God is that there's always so
much more to know, so much more to
discover. Just when we least expect it, he
intrudes into our neat and tidy notions
about who he is and how he works.

Joni Eareckson Tada

God may not always come
when we need Him, but
He will always be on time.

Alex Haley

We shall come one day to a
heaven where we shall gratefully
know that God's great refusals
were sometimes the true answers
to our truest prayer.

P. T. Forsyth

God is never late.

People are like stained glass windows; they sparkle and shine when the sun is out, but when the darkness sets in their true beauty is revealed only if there is a light within.

Elizabeth Kubler-Ross

Through many dangers, toils, and snares
we have already come;
'Twas grace that brought me safe thus far,
and grace will lead me home.

John Newton

Serenity is not freedom from the storm,
but peace during the storm.

I'll go where you want me to go, dear Lord, over mountain, or plain, or sea; I'll say what you want me to say, dear Lord, I'll be what you want me to be.

Mary Elizabeth Brown

It is for us to make the effort. The result is always in God's hands.

Mohandas K. Gandhi

With God as your partner, all things are possible.

Fifty years from now, it will not matter what kind of car you drove, what kind of house you lived in, how much you had in your bank account nor what your clothes looked like. But the world will be a little better because you were important in the life of a child.

Children are meant to be seen and heard and believed.

I have held many things in my hands, and I have lost them all; but whatever I have placed in God's hands, that I still possess.

Martin Luther

As we come to know Him better we shall spend more time in His presence and find that presence a constant and ever-increasing delight.

E. M. Bounds

I have a God of my very own, and wherever I am God is.

Faith is an oasis in the heart
which will never be reached
by the caravan of thinking.

Kahlil Gibran

Faith doesn't wait until it understands;
in that case it wouldn't be faith.

Vance Havner

Fear knocked at the door. Faith answered.
No one was there.

It is God to whom and with whom we travel,
and while he is the End of our journey,
he is also at every stopping place.

Elisabeth Elliot

A man should hear a little music, read a little
poetry, and see a fine picture every day of his
life, in order that worldly cares may not
obliterate the sense of the beautiful which
God has implanted in the human soul.

Johann von Goethe

We were not put on this earth by God
to make a living, but to make a life.

Deep within our consciousness is the realization
there is a Higher Power . . . our Lord and God.
That our life has a purpose, a destiny, a meaning,
a relationship which must be discovered and
developed. Until this is achieved you will experience
boredom, frustration, dissatisfaction. Only the
indwelling presence of this Power will satisfy
the hunger of your soul.

Alfred A. Montapert

To us also, through every star,
through every blade of grass,
is not God made visible if we will
open our minds and our eyes?

Thomas Carlyle

My job is to take care of
the possible and trust God
with the impossible.

It is not my business to think about myself.
My business is to think about God.
It is for God to think about me. *Simone Weil*

Experience is the dividend you get
from your mistakes.

James Russell Lowell

If nothing seems to go my way
today, this is my happiness:
God is my Father and I am his child.

Basilea Schlink

I am a precious fallible child of God.

If we are ever to enjoy life,
now is the time, not tomorrow or next year.
Today should always be our most wonderful day.

Thomas Dreier

Every day is my best day; this is my life,
I'm not going to have this moment again.

Bernie Siegel

If you really want to be happy, nobody can stop you.
Sister Mary Tricky

What you are doing I may not be able to do....
What I am doing you may not be able to do....
But all of us together are doing
something beautiful for God.

Mother Teresa

Snowflakes are one of
nature's most fragile things,
but just look what they can
do when they stick together.

Vesta M. Kelly

Together we can do most anything.

Religions are different roads converging upon the same point. What does it matter that we take different roads so long as we reach the same goal?

Gandhi

Only he who keeps his eye fixed on the far horizon will find his right road.

Dag Hammarskjold

There are many paths to God.

Into all our lives, in many simple, familiar, homely ways, God infuses this element of joy from the surprises of life, which unexpectedly brighten our days, and fill our eyes with light.

Samuel Longfellow

Our God is so wonderfully good and lovely and blessed in every way that the mere fact of belonging to him is enough for an untellable fullness of joy!

Hannah Whiteall Smith

It is not how much we have, but how much we enjoy, that makes happiness. *Charles Haddon Spurgeon*

Prayer is exhaling the spirit of man and inhaling the spirit of God.

Edwin Keith

People who pray for miracles usually don't get miracles. . . But people who pray for courage, for strength to bear the unbearable, for the grace to remember what they have left instead of what they have lost, very often find their prayers answered. . . . Their prayers helped them tap hidden reserves of faith and courage which were not available to them before.

Harold Kushner

The hands that help are holier
than the lips that pray.

Robert G. Ingersoll

Real prayer always does one of two things:
It either frees us from the trouble we fear,
or it gives us the strength and courage
to meet the trouble when it comes.

~101~

Prayer is the peace of our spirit,
the stillness of our thoughts,
the evenness of our recollection,
the sea of our meditation,
the rest of our cares,
and the calm of our tempest.

Jeremy Taylor

He who has learned to pray has learned
the greatest secret of a holy and happy life.

William Law

Don't bother to give God instructions; just report for duty.

Corrie Ten Boom

What we love to do we find time to do.

John Lancaster Spalding

God's will for us is our well being.

Let the beauty we love be what we do. There are
hundreds of ways to kneel and kiss the ground. *Rumi*

No one can arrive from being talented alone.
God gives talent;
work transforms talent into genius.

Anna Pavlova

The talents we are given are our gift from God.
How we use them is our gift to God.

A. Russo

Talent on loan from God.

When you have nothing left but God,
you become aware that God is enough.

Let nothing disturb you,
let nothing frighten you:
everything passes away except God;
God alone is sufficient.

St. Teresa of Avila

Relax, God is in charge.

Be simple; take our Lord's hand
and walk through things.

Fr. Andrew

He delights to meet the faith
of one who looks up to Him
and says, "Lord, you know
that I cannot do this — but I
believe that you can!"

Amy Carmichael

I can't. God can. I think I'll let God.

To get up each morning with
the resolve to be happy...
is to set our own conditions to
the events of each day.
To do this is to condition
circumstances instead of
being conditioned by them.

Ralph Waldo Trine

A joyful heart is like the sunshine of God's love.

Mother Teresa

Never walk when you can dance.
Marshall Rosenberg

At that place in life where
your talents meet the needs of
the world, that is where God
wants you to be.

Albert Schweitzer

He does most in God's great world
who does his best in his own little world.

Thomas Jefferson

The well of Providence is deep.
It's the buckets we bring to it that are small.

Mary Webb

It is not the number of books you read, nor
the variety of sermons you hear, but it is the
frequency and earnestness with which you
meditate on these things till the truth in them
becomes your own and part of your being,
that insures your growth.

F. W. Robertson

Love doesn't make the world go 'round.
Love is what makes the ride worthwhile.

Franklin P. Jones

If the world is cold,
make it your business to build fires.

Horace Traubel

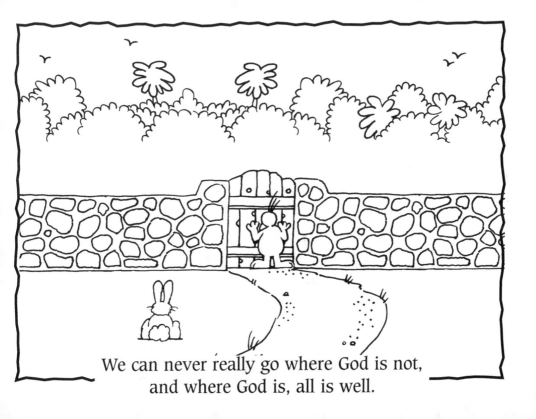

We can never really go where God is not,
and where God is, all is well.

It is amazing how lucky I
become whenever I consistently
put out my best effort.

Cybil Franklin

My obligation is to do the right thing.
The rest is in God's hands.

Martin Luther King

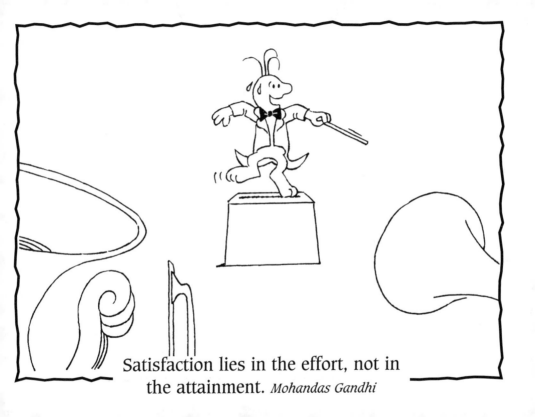

Satisfaction lies in the effort, not in the attainment. *Mohandas Gandhi*

From you I receive, to you I give.
Together we share, from this we live.

Rabbis Joseph and Nathan Siegel

A friend is one to whom one may pour
out all the contents of one's heart, chaff
and grain together, knowing that gentle
hands will take and sift it, keep what is
worth keeping, and with a breath of
kindness, blow the rest away.

George Eliot

Friendship is God's special way of
loving us through someone else.

When a man takes one step toward God,
God takes more steps toward that man
than there are sands in the worlds of time.

You never test the resources of God until
you attempt the impossible.

F. B. Meyers

If you want God to move a mountain,
you'd better bring a shovel.

There is great happiness in not wanting,
in not being something, in not going somewhere.

J. Krishnamurti

Life is not short; life is eternal, so there is no
question of any hurry. By hurrying you can
only miss. In existence do you see any hurry?
Seasons come in their time, flowers come in
their time, trees are not running to grow fast
because life is short. It seems as if the whole
of existence is aware of the eternity of life.

Osho

God grant me the serenity to accept the things I cannot change, the courage to change the things I can, and the wisdom to know the difference. *Reinhold Niebuhr*

No matter what age you are,
or what your circumstances might be,
you are special and still have
something unique to offer.
Your life, because of who you are,
has meaning.

Barbara De Angelis

Remember that you are unique.
If that is not fulfilled,
then something wonderful has been lost.

Martha Graham

I am God's melody of life.
God sings her song through me.

For peace of mind,
resign as general manager of the universe.

Larry Eisenberg

My mother always encouraged us
to keep moving forward with the words:
"If you take one step, God will take two."

Carrie P. Meek

The sole purpose of this human life is nothing but the realization of God. Meditate on Him with as much reverence and love as you can . . . . Forget all except Him. Speak to Him, "O God, bless me." Speak, cry, laugh, dance, do anything, let flow your ecstatic tears. From Him is this all. Without Him there is nothing . . . . Then a time will come when you will actually see Him before you. Your joy will know no bounds. Your ignorance, all this pleasure and pain will vanish. Your whole outlook will be changed.

The Shivapuri Baba

We can't help liking the preacher
who hands out calling cards with
this sentence printed on them:
"What on earth are you doing
for Heaven's sake?"

Mechtild of Magdeburg

Prayer is the burden of a sigh;
the falling of a tear;
the upward glancing of an eye,
when none but God is near.

James Montegomery

God is contagious. Catch God.

God will never let you be shaken or moved
from your place near His heart.

Joni Eareckson Tada

God danced the day you were born.

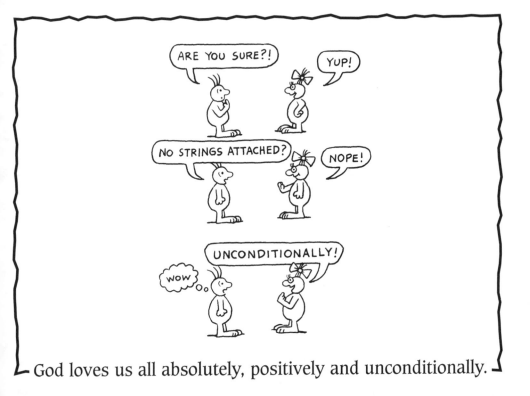

God loves us all absolutely, positively and unconditionally.

Sometimes you just have to take the leap,
and build your wings on the way down.

Kobi Yamada

Faith is continuing to run the race, assured
that you will get your second wind. Faith is
focusing on God's promises, and cropping out
the world's discouragements. Faith is
confidently expecting miracles from the
Source and Promiser of miracles.

William A. Ward

With God, anything is possible.

If we just give God the little that we have,
we can trust Him to make it go around.

Gloria Gaither

Faith is raising the sail of our little boat
until it is caught up in the soft winds
above and picks up speed,
not from anything within itself,
but from the vast resources
of the universe around us.

Ralph W. Ward, Jr.

The winds of grace blow all the time.
All we need to do is set our sails.

Ramakrishna

Children Need...

Appreciation, for all they bring into our lives.

Balance, somewhere between too little and too much.

Commitment, it's the little things we do each day that matter.

Dreams, to touch the future.

Empathy, remember what it was like to be a child.

Family and friends, everyone needs someone to love.

Guidance, actions speak louder than words.

Healthy habits, to nurture body, mind and spirit.

Inspiration, to explore beauty, wonder and mystery.

Joy, sprinkle laughter and happiness daily.

Kindness, to learn to care for others as they are cared for.

Limits, set boundaries and consequences together.

Mentors, to give wings to their aspirations.

Nature, to delight in rainbow butterflies and shooting stars.

Opportunities, to discover what truly makes their heart sing.

Play, the "work" of childhood.

Quiet time, to recharge their batteries.

Responsibilities, to build self-esteem and self-confidence.

Security, feeling safe is essential for growth.

Traditions, keep the family tree alive and sprout new branches.

Unconditional love, for who they are, not for what they do.

Values, live yours and encourage them to find theirs.

Words of encouragement, "You can do it, I believe in you."

Xoxoxo's, hug and kiss them each and every day.

You, your presence more than your presents.

Zzzzzzzs, a good night's sleep.

© Meiji Stewart

138

Children are God's apostles, sent forth, day by day,
to preach of love, and hope and peace. *James Russell Lowell*

God meets our needs in unexpected ways.

Janette Oke

God, to me, it seems,
is a verb.

R. Buckminster Fuller

Grow where you are planted. Begin to
weave and God will give you the thread.

German Proverb

God can't give you anything new
until you let go of the old.

Although we have been made to believe
that if we let go we will end up with nothing,
life itself reveals again and again the opposite:
that letting go is the path to real freedom.

Sogyal Rinpoche

Take time to be holy.

Howard Finster

I know this world is ruled by infinite intelligence....
Everything that surrounds us —
everything that exists —
proves that there are infinite laws behind it.
There can be no denying this fact.
It is mathematical in its precision.

Thomas A. Edison

Live in such a way that those who
know you but don't know God
will come to know God
because they know you.

Only in the sacredness of inward silence does
the soul truly meet the secret, hiding God.

Frederick William Robertson

Know God; know serenity. No God; no serenity.

If I have the belief that I can do it, I shall surely acquire the capacity to do it even if I may not have it at the beginning.

Mahatma Gandhi

If God sends us on stony paths, he provides strong shoes.

Corrie Ten Boom

Nothing is going to happen today
that God and I can't handle.

Explore daily the will of God.

Carl Jung

That we are alive today
is proof positive that God
has something
for us to do today.

Anna R. B. Lindsay

God's will is for you to go out and
do something for someone else.

When I pedal and let God steer, we really go places. When I steer I go in circles.

Some people are always telegraphing to Heaven for God to send a cargo of blessing to them, but they are not at the wharf side to unload the vessel when it comes.

F. B. Meyer

How come you're running around
looking for God? God isn't lost.

As children bring their broken toys, with tears for us to mend, I brought my broken dreams to God, because God is my friend. But then, instead of leaving God in peace to work alone, I hung around and tried to help with ways that were my own. At last, I snatched them back and cried "How could you be so slow?" "My child," God said "What could I do? You never did let go."

Let go and let God be in charge.

God put me on earth to accomplish a certain number of things. Right now I am so far behind, I will live forever.

Little gift books, big messages

Thought-provoking, attitude-changing wonderful recipes on how to make the best from the "wurst" of any situation. Accepting challenges and overcoming adversity can lead to greater self-esteem, self-acceptance and self-discovery.
Order No. 6460

A uniquely illustrated "you can if you think you can" book to empower anybody – student, co-worker, relative, friend, partner, child – to aspire to, believe in, and pursue their dreams. Go for it! Life is not a dress rehearsal.
Order No. 6456

Little gift books, big messages

The best survival kit for living and loving in the jungle of everyday life. Great line drawings and timeless truths to offer hope and encouragement for anyone facing the daily challenges of our fast-paced, stress-filled society.
Order No. 6458

Happiness is a choice. Pass it on! Really knowing we all have the power to choose happiness at any moment, in any situation, is truly empowering. This book is a great reminder that happiness is found right here, right now.
Order No. 6566

Little gift books, big messages

A wondrous gift for anybody interested in the well-being of children. This delightfully illustrated book uses wisdom from the ages and poignant humor to encourage everyone, especially parents and teachers, to love, cherish, and honor children.

Order No. 6457

Parenting, the ultimate adventure. Raising a child can be life's most demanding and extraordinary challenge and also its greatest happiness. A perfect gift for parents, grandparents, teachers and child care providers.

Order No. 6568

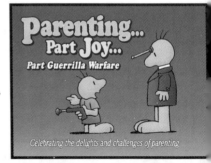

Little gift books, big messages

Dare to follow your heart's desire.... Dare to harvest your dreams.... Dare to speak your truth.... Dare to nurture your spirit.... An ideal gift book to encourage anybody to aspire to, believe in, and pursue dreams.
Order No. 6570

God has a purpose and a plan for you that no one else can fulfill. You are a miracle, unique and unrepeatable. Help someone celebrate their spiritual nature with this collection of empowering and loving wisdom.
Order No. 6569

These books are available from

1-800-328-9000
www.hazelden.org

About the Author

Meiji Stewart has created other gift books, designs, and writings that may be of interest to you. Please visit www.puddledancer.com or call 1-877-EMPATHY (367-2849) for more information about any of the items listed below.

(1) **Hazelden/Keep Coming Back** - Over two hundred gift products including greeting cards, wallet cards, bookmarks, magnets, bumper stickers, gift books, and more. (Free catalog available from Hazelden at 800-328-9000.)

(2) **ABC Writings** - Titles include *Children Are, Children Need, Creativity Is, Dare To, Fathers Are, Friends Are, Grandparents, Great Teachers, Happiness Is, I Am, Life Is, Loving Families, May You Always Have, Mothers Are, Recovery Is, Soulmates, Success Is,* and many more works in progress. Many of these ABC writings are available as posters (from Portal Publications) at your favorite poster and gift store, or directly from Hazelden on a variety of gift products.

(3) *Nonviolent Communication: A Language of Compassion* by Marshall Rosenberg. (from PuddleDancer Press) - Jack Canfield (*Chicken Soup for the Soul* author) says, "I believe the principles and techniques in this book can literally change the world – but more importantly, they can change the quality of your life with your spouse, your children, your neighbors, your co-workers, and everyone else you interact with. I cannot recommend it highly enough." Available from Hazelden and your local and on-line bookstores. For more information about The Center for Nonviolent Communication please visit www.cnvc.org.

◼ HAZELDEN®
Keep Coming Back™

Complimentary Catalog Available
Hazelden: P.O. Box 176, Center City, MN 55012-0176
1-800-328-9000   www.hazelden.org

Hazelden/Keep Coming Back titles available from your favorite bookstore:

Relax, God is in Charge	ISBN 1-56838-377-0
Keep Coming Back	ISBN 1-56838-378-9
Children are Meant to be Seen and Heard	ISBN 1-56838-379-7
Shoot for the Moon	ISBN 1-56838-380-0
When Life Gives You Lemons...	ISBN 1-56838-381-9
It's a Jungle Out There!	ISBN 1-56838-382-7
Parenting... Part Joy... Part Guerrilla Warfare	ISBN 1-56838-383-5
God Danced the Day You Were Born	ISBN 1-56838-384-3
Happiness is an Inside Job	ISBN 1-56838-385-1
Anything is Possible	ISBN 1-56838-386-X

Acknowledgements

Every effort has been made to find the copyright owner of the material used. However, there are a few quotations that have been impossible to trace, and we would be glad to hear from the copyright owners of these quotations, so that acknowledgement can be recognized in any future edition.

Hazelden Information and Educational Services is a division of the Hazelden Foundation, a not-for-profit organization. Since 1949, Hazelden has been a leader in promoting the dignity and treatment of people afflicted with the disease of chemical dependency.

The mission of the foundation is to improve the quality of life for individuals, families, and communities by providing a national continuum of information, education, and recovery services that are widely accessible; to advance the field through research and training; and to improve our quality and effectiveness through continuous improvement and innovation.

Stemming from that, the mission of this division is to provide quality information and support to people wherever they may be in their personal journey—from education and early intervention, through treatment and recovery, to personal and spiritual growth.

Although our treatment programs do not necessarily use everything Hazelden publishes, our bibliotherapeutic materials support our mission and the Twelve Step philosophy upon which it is based. We encourage your comments and feedback.

The headquarters of the Hazelden Foundation is in Center City, Minnesota. Additional treatment facilities are located in Chicago, Illinois; New York, New York; Plymouth, Minnesota; St. Paul, Minnesota; and West Palm Beach, Florida. At these sites, we provide a continuum of care for men and women of all ages. Our Plymouth facility is designed specifically for youth and families.

For more information on Hazelden, please call **1-800-257-7800**. Or you may access our World Wide Web site on the Internet at **www.hazelden.org**.